Introdu

To be honest, I'm actually amazed that I have come to that moment I find myself writing a whole book, a book to be published and made available not only locally but globally. I was born with a condition called Cerebral Palsy which affects the body functions of my hands, therefore, as a child, I struggled at school because I was not able to hold a pen to write with my hands, but I was very intelligent. With that in mind, as I look back over the years, being told now and again that I can not write, before everyone else joins the party, let me be the first one to be proud of myself, I am amazed and feel so happy that I am actually sitting here writing a book.

I am into ICT profession, I have a Diploma in Information and Communication Technology, I occupy that space with ease and comfort, everywhere else it's really a struggle for me. Its complexity and vastness, intensity and depth is what always ignites my passion and interest for it even if I feel I have not gone as far in pursuing it as I could have as far as educational path can go, me and technology have a deep mutual understanding of one another and it is a long term relationship, I was introduced to computers, and other gadgets as assistive devices and technologies, at a very tender age in my early years of schooling when I was struggling with my disability as a child and has been my destiny helper since then. God and technology have conspired together to make the impossible possible, the one who could not write has written a book!

Information and Communication Technology is when we look into the technologies used to handle communications and information, processing and management. It is all about information getting from point A to point B right on time, received by the right person and the recipient being able to understand the information and what action to take on it, otherwise if any problems arise during this process, information is likely to fail to achieve the intended goal or objective. Back then, before the use of technology, there were a lot of communication barriers, the timelines were affected due to length of time taken to deliver the letters and get the response instantly or in real-time, the action to take could get affected due to absence of direct and effective communication between the sender and the receiver. We thank God for invention and innovation, everyone who has contributed to the invention of these new technologies we enjoy today deserves a round of applause from us all. Communication is now direct and instant, with all these instant messaging platforms we no longer wait to hear that sound of a honking bell of the postman's bike with a letter from mum saying she is coming next week only to find that it was written the previous week which means she should be coming this week any day, now WhatsApp is doing wonders for us, mum just sends a text like, "I'm on my way, I will be arriving in 15 minutes," Isn't that awesome?

Ok, enough of that, this book is not about technology, you must be wondering what was that all about. Well, I have decided to share with you some of my moments of mindful thinking, (I'm not sure exactly what to call it), my personal reflection about life, maybe my personal awakening journey or my spiritual journey. You know, we, as humans, have those moments of self-winding where we find ourselves questioning life, who we are in this life, seeking to understand our unique truest identity in the midst of the whole magnificent universe of life that waits patiently for us to realize, explore and actualize it. This moment of realization could be what Jesus Christ experienced when he was in the wilderness for forty days fasting, encountering the devil questioning him about his identity, if you are the Son of interview. Even when Mary got pregnant, she had that conversation or dialogue

What Is On The Other Side

Mollen Garikai

Published by Mollen Garikai, 2023.

WHAT IS ON THE OTHER SIDE

First edition. January 15, 2023.

ISBN: 979-8215895160

Written by Mollen Garikai.

Table of Contents

To Myself, Molly the beautiful soul that dwells in my body.

Also to everyone who have walked this journey with me.

Thank you for believing and enduring it all trusting and anticipating what we're becoming.

Trust me the reward will be awesome.

that helped her realize *that* she was filled with grace and became aware of herself for the first time.

That moment of awakening to yourself, "you" awakening to "You", meaning your physical senses or rather your mind becoming aware of your higher-self, and all you can do is to say yes and let this 'You' have its own way in you.

I personally feel that there is this deep longing within ourselves to come to full blown knowledge of our true essence of being, we need the veil to be removed so that we see things as they are in reality, not in part as we do now, like what Paul says to the believers in Corinth, "For we know in part... but when the completeness comes, the part disappears... For now we see only a reflection as in a mirror... Now I know in part, then I shall know fully, even as I am fully known." (1 Corinthians 13:9-12). Even to the Romans he says, "Not only so, but we ourselves... groan inwardly as we eagerly wait for our adoption to sonship, the redemption of our bodies." (Romans 8:23) What if we now no longer have to groan and wait but just awaken to ourselves to these bodies and see them in their own realities. I believe, this would be the beginning of life itself, in a way this would be the beginning of self-empowered people where we begin to live life with a better understanding of who we are and what we are supposed to be doing with ourselves in this world.

We might be here in existence with all capabilities, potential and the zeal to make it in life, but not knowing what, when, where, why, how should we do will always hinder us to achieve our objectives, our missions and purposes in this life, we will even miss the timelines, chances and opportunities that were made available for us before time, due to lack of knowledge or understanding. Without understanding, we remain stagnant, we are like a car engine that fails to start, it continues idling instead of turning the ignition on and off we go, for understanding puts all things together and paves the way for everything else to fall into the rightful places and right on time. Somewhere in the bible is written that my people die because they lack knowledge, knowing is the first step towards achieving anything in life, you can only realize and do something you are aware of it and you learn to understand it so that you can actualize it. That is where information comes into play, information is critical and needs to be communicated effectively in order to take action. Seek ye first the kingdom of God and everything else will be added unto you, in other words, pursue knowledge and everything else will fall into place as you grow in understanding things pertaining to life.

Allow me to use technological illustration here. How do we come to know or become aware of something? Like a computer that receives instructions from the outside environment, we also receive information externally through the sensory system, sight, touch, hearing, taste and smell, outside ourselves, we have to see something, hear, taste, smell touch something to translate it as information or instruction. It is sent to the brain and the job of the brain is to download and send it to the mind where it is processed through discernment, decisions, understanding and making sense, it is stored in memory as thoughts, then printed out as actions, reactions, response, feedback or communicated to the outer world or environment for others to see and experience it from a personal point of connection. Therefore, processed information is what brings transformation, we can only do something once file transfer has been completed and sent to the right mind with an ability to process and bring forth the capability to act upon what has been communicated. At the end of the whole process we will need to see the output, the processed message. You might have missed my point there but don't worry, deeper details are coming as we go.

I am writing this book with an intention to help myself, and others who will resonate, to come into a better understanding of what life is all about. Life appears to many of us as something outside of ourselves, whereby we kind of wait upon or reach out to external forces to make it happen, Yes most of us we believe in God or the Supreme non-physical being but we are not fully convinced about it and we find ourselves going back and forth, not sure what to know and do about God, we feel like this Being is a world of endless mystery where he enjoys to play hide and seek, he is an equation difficult to simplify. But what if we are the ones who overthink and complicate things? Maybe we are just not conscious of our true life where we fully reside in true reality of life just like God. Remember we are created in his own image and we are like him in the Spirit form. We are only aware and confined in our physical bodies and live for the outer world.

I am taking this time to let you into my small yet the most beautiful part of my world, my corner of reflection, my prayer mountain, my alter and my point of connection to life, where I spend almost 95% part of my day most of the time, if not all the time. Someone is saying, you must have nothing to do in life for you to have so much time apportioned to reflection. Yes, I have all the time for that due to my life circumstances, and no, reflection is not really about time, it is a continuous conversation you do with yourself within.

As I take you on this small amazing spiral level of awakening adventure, my intention is to see people changing their perspective towards life, the point of view is very critical. At times we fail dismally due to the positions from which we are looking at things. During the time of Moses, there was a time when people were required to just look at the serpent for them to be saved, maybe some died because they were disadvantaged by the sitting arrangements, they were sitting at a further distance away from where the serpent was hanging that the serpent was not visible enough to look at. Maybe we are just too far from where the reality is taking place or we are too close that the picture is very wide and clear, so the angle of view is very important.

There is a perspective which can do away with distance and space so that we can look at life with clarity. We are required to find ourselves, define who we are, discover ourselves and purposes, find the resources and tools available for us, and master the ability to achieve the intended goal, as well as not to just pursue our dreams and purposes, but to reach the pinnacle of our potential, to go above and beyond for we all have the ability and capacity to get there.

I want to put a **DISCLAIMER** before we dive into the deep waters. Like I said before, this is a record of my personal life experiences and reflections, I do not intend to make you think highly of me as someone who knows it all, or who have made it in life, I'm still struggling with some of the things mentioned in here. Neither am I trying to convince you of anything, but maybe I might succeed in convincing you to reimagine life and fully occupy your space.

You do not need to think too much, overthinking will only destroy this beautiful space I am seeing and take away some lessons in it that might help you along the way to your own place of truth. I urge you to allow it to just flow and resonate if possible. I have no perfect reason why you should take the contents of this book seriously and trust them to make sense to you and work in your life but I can also assure you that it will help you get going from where you are to the next level of faith. Knowledge will always abound from glory to glory in a continuous spiral shift of life, from faith to faith because life is eternal, it continues to expand its circles as we pursue it, that's how it is spiral. Therefore, my hope is to find you along the way as I continue with my journey giving you what I found in the inner depths during my season of inner world adventures.

THE BOOK LAYOUT:

- This is a spiritual book inspired by the Word from the Christian bible, therefore every chapter will start with a verse to reflect on in line with the chapter titles.
- Second part is where I share my personal reflections as it is enlightened from a spiritual understanding and inspiration.
- Then, in one or two chapters, I will share my personal life experiences to practically motivate and inspire someone who

will resonate with the message in that chapter.

- In closing, there is a guided meditation prayer to help someone to spiritually align the body, mind and soul to the deep things of God as the Spirit leads us.

Chapter One
The Law of Contrast

"For if you live according to the flesh, you will die; but if by the Spirit you put to death the misdeeds of the body, you will live" (Rom 8.13)

Have you ever wondered how it happened? Life just happened? How did we get here? If we, for a moment, assume God is out of the equation, then how did a drop of human tissue came into being? How did it find itself swimming inside a water bag for 9 months, and upon arrival, found itself surrounded by intelligence and everything started working out and falling into place just like that? Really? No, I don't think so. There should be something bigger happening behind the scenes beyond this life. In as much as there are some people who are still yet to believe in God, the Supreme Being or super power, the non-physical power, the real evidence of this power is in the nature where we see natural events taking place with no one close to home officially launching them, we see clouds forming themselves, filling themselves with water and in no time we see them emptying themselves and filling rivers and streams with water in due season, we see birds flocking around in the air, we wouldn't even know where they are heading or coming from and on what mission, we put seeds in the ground but germination process and ability to produce is beyond us.

With all the evidence that we see around us in the physical world, we conclude that there is the unseen world around us as well. We do not see it because we cannot see what we are not aware of , in other words we only realize what we become aware of, we awaken as we come into the knowledge of something. Therefore, the unseen will only become visible as we are awakened to it. There is that Bigger Power that exists somewhere, we might differ on what names we give it, God, Christ, Allah, Universe and so on, names do not matter, they are just identifiers we needed to label and tag on to it so that we are able to talk about it as we refer to it, but they are all one and the same thing contextually.

So now we have two worlds in existence, visible, the one we see, and the invisible, hence, the dualistic aspect of life. Duality or contrast is a spiritual law that governs the universe which states that everything has a complementary opposite within the whole self or in the sameness, like a coin with two sides, head and tail, or hot and cold situation where there is only the varying degrees in temperature. Everything we know in this life is sitting in alternating angles of the other. This is how we are able to compare and contrast between things, to pass judgement on situations and circumstances. Good is better because of bad, we live to die, there is coming and going, we have failure on this side and success on the other side, we rise and then fall, light and dark. The Preacher in Ecclesiastes 3 says there is time for everything, they all happen in due season. At times that going back and forth makes life meaningless and realize that all is vanity or illusion, nothing is happening in reality. We are more like moving in a meandering stream where things keep changing as life flows from one bend over to the other. A new baby is born in the house while somewhere across the street a friend loses a loved one, he got a job last week but someone resigned or got fired, she got married recently and her boss divorced a few months ago. Events are happening to everyone regardless from what angles or times they are taking place, when you get employment you are in a season of employment so enjoy the fun of working and all that comes with it, you will be out of season someday.

Duality is what gives us the ability to see and discern things as this life is happening, it becomes the key element of our ability to reason as human beings, to define or distinguish things by spotting the difference. We are able to identify what we want from what we do not want, we can see where we are and what we do not have so that we can stir and initiate some desire and develop an ambition to go towards a new realization and manifest it. Difficulties and hardships help us to realize, acknowledge and appreciate better circumstances than the hardships, loneliness helps to magnify and value friendship, you can learn to love from the place of absence of it, it is only when you are lonely when you miss your friend and decide to appreciate him better next you see him again.

So all the compare and contrast we do is what helps us to want better, is what ignites that desire for more and better. Desire is stirred from within for the purpose to evolve and expand towards inner satisfaction which is the ultimate intention of all that we desire, to be satisfied at the end of it all.

As much as it is a good thing to have this ability to discern, contrasting cause conflicts because at times our perceptions are biased depending on the point of view or the position from which we see things, at times it is impossible to see both sides relatively or from both ends at the same place or time, it is an 'either-or' situation, you are either on one end or on the other and you do not have a full view of the situation, you are either here or there. We will have to develop the ability to go above the environment for us to see from a higher point of view, like an eagle that soars to a highest position in the sky to strategically see what is happening on the ground, that is why it will never miss its target.

I see God as this big giant, super power somewhere up and above beyond the whole galaxy of heavens where he watches from the highest point of view and his judgement is truth and righteous because he has the ability or capacity to see , not in part but the whole picture of what is happening as events take place.

The inability to be on top of the situation to see the full picture and understand that we are in the continuous state of the same is what causes conflicts, wars are a result of conflicting views, collective consciousness of two countries failing to resolve conflicts due to the inability to see from the enemy's camp side. In other words, thinking differently is what causes war. Misunderstandings are caused by the other not having a full view of the other side involved in order to understand it fully, they are fighting for their own truth they are seeing on their sides relatively. The conflict can only be resolved when they decide to give up on their own ego and try to see the other side or merge the sides into one situation to resolve based on what is on the ground to save the whole bigger picture of the subjects involved.

So duality is the law of relativity and contrast is there to bring balance into a continuous flow of things. I will say this again, life is like a meandering stream that remains in continuous state of flow until it reaches the next bend caused by some boulders or rocks it encounters along the way of its flow then it starts another state of flow, but the flow remains constant as long as it is connected to its source.

Therefore, ups and downs, valleys and mountains, hot and cold, joy and sadness, knowledge and ignorance are all part of the bigger picture but balance only comes when we become aware and have full knowledge of this bigger picture of life. Knowing what you do not want gives you information about what you want,. Knowing what is over here will always show you what is over there, it is relativity at play. The contrast helps us to become aware of what is and what is not so that we are inspired to have a desire to close the gap between the two for us to experience the whole.

Having established the law of duality, now let us go back to my question I asked in the beginning. How did we get here? How did it happen that we exist in this life? To be honest, there are trillions of concepts and theories on that subject to which some sound weird, like the animal evolution and all that, I personally do not want to believe but at the same time when I see some behaviors of other human beings I tend to wonder if that theory of evolution.

I am a devoted Christian, the story of creation in the bible, to some extent, tries to get to the deepest deep of the origins of life. That narrative goes deep into the woods of the beginning, but I feel that the creation story on its own just brings the latter part where we see God forming the physical world, the visible realm of existence, where life is governed by sensory system we touch it, taste, hear, see and smell things, when we lose all these abilities we are pronounced dead. What then is beyond this non-physical setup? There should be a part that comes before, after and beyond this reality in Genesis story of physical creation, the 'beyond beginning' is the missing piece of the puzzle that we are looking for to understand this life, the unseen world that exists before and beyond time and space. I want the infinite or eternal life that exists outside the confinements of this physical world that we are more conscious or aware of. I think this physical world is just a tiny place where we pass by for a moment as we move around in the spaces and realms of life with all that its beautiful environment and vastness we see and experience in this life. It does not make sense to be here just for seventy year and be done with it if there is no other places or life beyond this one. What is the purpose of this world then?

The moment we realize or become aware of the non-physical world is the beginning of wisdom in true essence, its vastness, intensity and depth, life in abundance. That is what my mind has been playing around and questing to understand.

Life begins in the knowledge of why you are here, who you are, where you are, what you are doing and how you are living, knowing your place and purpose gives meaning to life. Most people are just in the mere existence of life, moving up and down the streets with eyes opened but blind to life, not being aware of the fullness of life they have at their disposal. Knowing and understanding life awakens the purpose of it in us, the ability to live the best and beyond, the potential is activated and the engine is ignited for the journey of life to begin.

WHAT IS ON THE OTHER SIDE

We all have that desire to know our place or have that sense of belonging so that we live a purpose-driven lifestyle or mindset. Being aware of your identity leads you to purpose and living that purpose consciously will always take you to where your resources and toolkits are. Everything and everyone in your life become cooperative components working with you to accomplish your purpose. He who gave you the purpose and assignment for that mission to be accomplished also supplied the resources and game-plan in order to accomplish it. You are not alone in this, your purpose is as critical as anyone else's therefore do not downplay it no matter your circumstances around you.

As uniquely and individually assigned to each one of us, all our purposes are also working collectively together to fulfill the eternal destiny, that is why I feel it is very important to be aware of what life is all about, it speeds up and fuels the efforts being put on the individual level and the performance will further help the whole system to move forward and faster in its growth and expansion. We need to be well informed for us to understand what and how to live life, once we are aligned to assignment then the show can now begin.

I intend to share with you some insights on how I now view life from another angle of perspective which is outside the ordinary. Please always note that this is me sharing my thoughts and my reflections about life, I do not intend to confuse you or divert you from your way of understanding. Let's just loosen our minds a bit and have fun, the writer and the reader have just met on one of those mutual moments where one has to do what needs to be done on this side whilst the other performs on the other side, remember the law of relativity, the author of a book needs a reader for her book. Just read with an open mind to receive an understanding that can freely lead you to another place of understanding. Please note that this is not about religion, I will make reference to the bible scriptures because my reflections are inspired by the Word, you do not understand religiously but spiritually. Travel this journey with me, let us walk it with ease at heart, open to another understanding, another way of looking at life!

Life Experience

When I was born, my physical body was fine and 'normal' like any other new born baby, but my mother said I was too small and weighted less than normal baby weight. After about four days after birth, I got ill with yellow fever and it developed into what they call infant jaundice, commonly known as yellow fever, which occurs because the baby's blood contains an excess of bilirubin, a yellow pigment of the red blood cells. This is commonly caused by an underlying disease or condition like when the baby's liver is not mature enough to get rid of this yellow pigment from the bloodstream, high blood level of bilirubin can put a newborn baby at risk of severe jaundice which causes brain damage.

That's how I got Cerebral Palsy, a motor disability caused by abnormal brain damage to the developing brain that affects the ability to control the muscles. That was the physical body that my soul occupied. My soul is in there as the life unfolds while the body continued to develop and grow into a child despite this physical body condition. I would like to think that, my soul, which is the real 'me', the spiritual being coming into this world, was very much aware of the space and was so ready to occupy it. As an infant, I'm sure the baby is not very much into the outside environment, it mainly focuses on what keeps the physical body alive, liquids and fluids, feeding the body and crying out for more growth. In about 9-12 months, the sensory body system should be fully developed and ready to get started with life. During this period, the soul is more alive than the physical body, it lives in the within-ness world where nothing else matters as long as body and soul are still together in this life.

I don't think I was even aware of the condition as a baby, all was good because I was still learning and adjusting to the environment, figuring out how this body is going to work. So I failed to meet many expected physical body functions development, I could not sit when I was expected to sit on my own, I did not crawl on time, and I ended up not walking in my entire physical life. My speech ability kicked in very late and I still have it jumbled at times with inaudible words. Many of the basic abilities came through slowly with time, it was like persuading them to show up by negotiating my way to them, discovering them one by one from inside.

Despite this condition, the real 'me' was inside sitting pretty and cozy inside this body without judging it for the soul is more alive to its purpose and mission than the physical body, especially in the early years of life. Whilst I continued to grow, I reached a stage where I could hear, smell, touch, see and talk, the sensory system, sight was just fine but I had squinty eyes, hearing and smelling were perfectly fine, touching which is also the sense of feeling was also good because I could feel my whole body from inside and out. Therefore, this was a good start, the whole sensory system was almost perfect to enable the body to function. The problem was the connectivity between the functions of the brain and the body limbs. Outwardly the body is perfect, nothing looks disfigured or displaced, I have the most beautiful body structure that some women admire enviously.

There is a discord between the brain and the body caused by the brain damage due to infant jaundice. The body is not fully connected and aligned to the brain in order to develop the ability to receive instructions from the brain to perform some of the functions, nothing is wrong with body but the brain has been experiencing some technical fault so the system is performing with limitations and I have no choice but to work with what I have.

But don't forget that I am not outside the house, the body, I have teen inside since the house was under construction. My soul accepted it even with the faulty brain.

However, the noise came from outside. The external environment made demands for the body to start living life, I would do things differently at my own pace and negotiate how I can do and adapt to my own way of doing things. The outside world is what gave me pressure and made me realize that things were not okay, My family consulted various doctors and spiritualists seeking to understand the situation to no avail. I was known as a child who was not 'normal', child with special needs, a disabled person, but my favorite term I came to know later on in life is 9differently abled person'. When people see me as differently abled, I feel fully accepted and accommodated in a world I am trying to fit in. It means I am not disabled from the world but enabled differently and all is working out but differently.

I am in the space in-between. My soul resides in this body so that it can access and interact with the world in order to experience and express the life of God physically. The soul is in-between the Spirit of God, the creator where life is coming from, and the physical body, where it uniquely experiences life as it showcase that endless possibilities of God's life as he experience himself in you. The soul is an individual being with a free will to experience life whatever you way it wants so it is up to an individual to work with the Spirit of God or to abandon the will of God.

The physical conditions and circumstances are not always supposed to be exactly what is expected in the world, the physical body is a temporary vehicle which is there to move around with the passenger and the car can also be going around with no headlights or a cracked window. Some cars are posche and elegant serving the purpose of luxurious lifestyle, some are chauffeur-driven to serve executive people. What differentiates these cars from each other are the purposes they are serving, but the main goal for all of them is to gas it up and get going. As long as there is still fuel in the tank nothing else matters. So it is with life, we are all different depending on our purposes and what is important to all of us is life, the breathing in and out, the fuel in the tank, nothing else matters.

In the next chapter we look at how we awaken to the things pertaining to life for us to understand how to integrate our physical bodies to the spirit of God for the soul to live to its purpose.

Personal Reflection Exercise

a) Find a quiet place and sit comfortably.

b) Close your eyes. Take a deep breath in and slowly breathe out, feel your body relax. Do it at least 3 times.

c) With your eyes closed, feel yourself inside your body. You see blackness before your eyes but as you relax whilst you breathe in and out your mind will eventually slide into the beyond and see other colors, random shapes waves or anything. The longer you linger in that space, the more you feel relaxed and free.

d) Breath is life, it is what God breathed into the body for it be alive when he created a man. So breathing is a path we can take that leads to your inner temple. Being aware of your breath is acknowledging and becoming aware of your life that lives in your body. Relaxing helps you to find a place to comfortably before the throne room of God, to worship and pray to him while he puts in your spirit the things you need for the day. Let your spirit collect the daily bread, the heavenly manna that the Israelites collected in the wilderness.

e) Say your prayers. And slowly bring back your senses to your breath and slowly open your eyes.

Chapter 2
The Power of Awareness

"Know ye not that ye are the temple of God, and that the Spirit of God dwelleth in you?
1 Corinthians 3.16

As I was writing about creation, there is a part that came to my mind from the narration of what happened in the garden of Eden in the early chapters of Genesis, whereby God, after creating everything in the land and the man was put in charge of everything, he gave a command that a man can eat anything else in the garden except this particular fruit of a tree within the garden, behold everything else was good but there was a tree and its fruits that was forbidden. For now I am not really interested in the context of that scene, I can write another book on that, I want to look into the idea of the tree, and its fruits.

The conception of a tree is in the seed that is sown into the ground, it germinates and we see it surfacing from the ground underneath then it continues to form itself into a tree with branches and leaves. If it is an apple tree, after leaves we expect to then see the flowers all over the tree, they forerun the coming of the fruits, in this case, the apples. The endgame of this process from the seed up to the leaves is the apples falling from the tree, and the cycle starts all over again. The mission is to produce apples, and if the production does not take place the tree is condemned for its barrenness that it can be cut off, pruned or even uprooted. People can help the tree to produce by watering, nurturing the tree by putting manure and all the efforts and methods they know, those efforts on the ground play a very vital role in the process of production but they can just be on the surface, that is the furthest they can go, the rest is up to the tree for it to produce based on its will and capacity.

But now that is the visible part of the life of this tree on the surface, the physical life in sensory dimension where we can see, touch, feel, hear, taste and smell as it goes about its daily toils living day and night to produce fruits. We have no idea what is going on underneath the surface and yet, with no doubt, the real work is happening underground, this is where the whole system is setup and functions from. Unfortunately we cannot see anything, maybe we could try to open the ground for us to do the tour on the bottom industrial site, I would expect to see a lot going on, ants and worms pouring buckets of chemicals and fossils to regulate the whatever alkaline in the soil for it to be good enough for the seed. We would contaminate the whole system and disturb the production if we open the ground to see the work, we will have to be extra careful if we are to take chances to peep into the ground underneath otherwise there will not be any tree to produce the fruits for us.

The process is launched from underneath, the seed is planted from outside but it has to be accepted in the ground for the assignment to be accomplished.

So we have the roots underneath the ground then the tree above the ground. Without roots there is no tree, without roots and tree there are no fruits, all the three elements or stages make up the tree life whole and complete from below and above, within and without, all are working together for the good of the tree, working towards achieving its purpose which is to produce the fruits, the expected outcome, in other words, what is coming out of the whole process – the manifestation.

I will assume that, down in the roots is where everything is layered out, planned, controlled and determined, the capacity of the roots determines the potential of the tree to produce the fruits, if the roots are contaminated or are sickly and infectious, then the whole system is affected. The tree depends on the strength of the roots for it to remain rooted, grounded and standing no matter the influence of the external forces around it. The roots carry the seed prototype of the expected fruits, the tree should develop the ability to draw strength from the deep, to go deeper into the moisture underneath reaching out to the water table for it to remain moisturized. The roots regulates the intake of nutrients it gets from the soil to meet the required specifications of the system for it to activate the capacity and ability to function in order to produce the expected results. Naturally the tree will just do what needs to be done and we will begin to see the growth taking place on the surface and in no time we will be collecting the fruits.

Not being aware of the roots and in the right alignment with the system underneath, the tree will also fail to produce on the surface, failure to comply with the roots, the tree will fail to perform and eventually falls down and dies. Failure to identify itself in the roots, the tree will not live to its best potential, the roots connects it to the source of life for it to maintain its capacity to hold the whole system together. Therefore, the roots are the deeper inner core of the tree and its mandate is to influence the tree from inside to fulfill its purpose.

It is like what happens with the egg, if an egg is broken by an outside force its life ends, we fry the egg and enjoy the breakfast and will not talk about the egg ever again, but if It is broken from inside, life begins, we will witness another level of life of egg in a chicken and it can grow and be able to produce more other eggs twice or more times in its lifetime. Greater things always begin from inside.

There are times when the tree fails to deliver expected results, and we curse that tree for not bearing fruits. It is the tree that we curse and no one mentions the roots because we barely see the roots and their functions, we are not so conscious or aware of them even if we subconsciously know of their importance, tree life cycles can go by without ever bringing the roots to the mind. But then when you sit down to deliberately think and understand, when you get to the point where you ask yourself what could be the 'root cause' of this outcome, that is when the tree starts to realign, becoming aware of the inner depths where the resources to learn and cultivate its ability to function as a tree were deposited when the seed was planted. It is wrong to concentrate and curse the fruits for not coming forth the way it was expected before checking underneath as well.

Even with the computer system, if you type a document and print out the hard copy then you realize there is an error, do you rub off the typo on the paper and take a new plain sheet and go ahead to print the document on the computer expecting the error to be gone? No, the error is on the software or the soft copy, you correct the document on the computer and then you print out, now you will have the correct document printed out as it is on the computer, as it is inside, so it is outside.

In this illustration of the roots and the tree, I am trying to point out that, we too as humans, have both the surface and the inner deep, we have the physical body and the inner body what is normally referred to as Soul and/or Spirit body. The physical body is what we are familiar with or more aware of, what is seen on the surface of the sensory dimension, we are more conscious of what we see, touch, taste, hear and smell. We exist in the five sensory dimension, these are used as a temporary interface between the inner and outer worlds as we experience the physical realm for a little while. The spiritual body is the inner being, the higher-self, the soul that enters the physical, or in other words, the physical body covers the soul as it exists inside. This soul is a separate entity that can exist outside the physical body, beyond the vastness of life, beyond time and space where it transcends beyond the feelings, the emotions and experiences. The spirit is designed and created to perform above and beyond our physical abilities, it is the one that comes into this world on a mission using the natural body to perform its purpose. It is wired and programmed with all the information, the required specifications, the tools and resources, the project plan, mission statements, goals and objectives, dreams and visions, the mandate and purposes pertaining to life. The 'you' that is put on 'You' should be aligned to the 'You' in 'you' in order to know and understand why 'You' are here.

All that we need is reserved inside waiting for the outer world, the physical body, to become aware of it, to come and reason together in alignment with the depth and discover it, have access to the Source in order to unleash the potential. It is like what we do with our radios, we tune in by choosing the right frequency or wavelength, aligning the radial to the radio station we want to listen to, if you do not fine tune the frequency to pick the frequency, you are likely to get crocky and inaudible sound.

Just like with the fruits, normally we curse what we see, when we perform below our potential because our focus is on the surface, we do not reach out to the inner world to check if we are still together in doing this life. If both worlds are relatively in sync with each other, aligned and immersed into one another in the sameness of life as it continues to flow from the Source of life to manifest his glory through us. It becomes a world of endless possibilities, we become supernatural beings who are empowered to perform beyond our abilities and limitations in this life.

With that realization of the two sided being, the dualism of life, my next question is how do we become aware of the other side, how do we bring that reality home in this sensory dimension, when does that wake up call come through?

We are all in this process of evolving everyday and asking these big questions is the beginning of wisdom. To me questions are always accompanied with their answers, the answers are built-in on the chip of the question. The moment I get a question in my mind, the next thing that comes to mind is the answer, at times it takes quite a while to figure out the answer but the longer I stay there and ponder on it is the closer I get to it. Those are my moments of cracking the codes and demystifying the mysteries, stepping into the unknown moment in order to remove that veil of ignorance one more time as my eyes of understanding are revealed to yet another stream of knowledge. Did you know that just one thought or idea that comes to mind brings along with it so many possibilities related to it? The longer you linger in the space of the unknown the more you create possibilities and are awakened to other realities you were not aware of.

In the next chapter, lets dive deeper into how the power of duality works and how to awaken to what is on the other side of the other, overcoming and becoming our own unique expressions of God.

Life Experience

I became fully aware of my disability when I started school, that's when I started to question my abilities because when I was home, help was always available without asking for it, everything was done for me by my mother and sister or anyone around. They were there all the time that, for me, that was a normal life because I was still a child, all that mattered was being alive to play and have fun. Of course I lived in an environment where life was not perfect, my parents were separated and we were staying with our mother's family so it was not a comfortable situation but for me, as a child, I was too young to worry about that.

I attended my elementary school at a boarding school and I remember I would cry every time my mother leaves me there. It was a new environment where I lived with new people who were not personally involved in my life so I feel like I was left there to discover myself with the help of the professionals who were experts as far as disability issues are concerned. That time is when I began to feel different from other people but it felt good that I was not the only one since it was a school for children with disabilities, it was not a big deal.

Because assistance was not readily available for me as it was at home, I started trying things out on my own, I also attended therapy sessions and trainings to help me bring out my abilities. Also questions began to come through as I wondered why my body is not working properly like others, I was contrasting my abilities with others' abilities and I would try some by working with possibilities available. The power of awareness lies in the contrast, we can only become aware when we notice something, depending on how we are attracted to it, either we launch a desire for it or we despise it.

I desired to improve on my abilities to the extent of using my sister to carry the burden. I would observe people doing things I couldn't do and let my mind learn where my hands could not work it out and, when I went home, I would teach her how things are done. I believe she is the most intelligent human being in my world because at my the age of four, she was able to understand my communication and would learn things from a person who was not capable of doing them. I remember she was able to write on the ground copying me writing on the ground with my toes and I would help her use hands to write with a color crayon. I also taught her how to sew and knit her dolls, as well as plaiting hair. She learnt a lot and matured earlier, and the best part was she believed in me, she is one person in this world who never misinterpreted her role to play in my life, she is so much aware of her responsibility and so aligned to her place no matter what is happening in her life.

That's how I grew, I learnt to accept my myself as a physically challenged child and I was blessed with corporate components the universe would always create for me to go through life. My soul had to accept my body and teach it how to negotiate its way of living and be aware of the endless possible solutions to the challenges. But the soul was always reaching out for more, believing in making things better, that at certain instances, solutions tried on my cases would work and be used for the whole school system or as part of the rehabilitation program. I was the first one to use a typewriter for writing in school because I could not write with my hands, I was the first one to wear a uniform with straps instead of buttons because I could not button up, I had a special chair where I would sit to balance as I used my typewriter so that it does not fall when I start having uncontrollable body shaking and involuntary muscle movements. I was also one of the first people to learn to use a computer in school when they were introduced since I was already familiar with typing and printing, and then at some point I also used a head-pointer for typing, whereby a long stick was technically put on my forehead and I would move the stick with my head to press the keys on the keyboard, I was the fastest computer student that time. So you see how the universe worked things out for me as I was defining my identity, my challenges would bring out solutions and I began to see myself wanting more so I kept pursuing my desires one after the other.

There was a point in life where I would have questions concerning life, the most common one was, why am I disabled? Who caused it and why? In trying to get answers, I would listen to conversations around, people discussing about me which was difficult to understand and come up with a helpful conclusion. My soul was so patient and very alert that I would collect what was good enough for its awakening towards the light of God, which is the knowledge of the Spirit life of God the Father. This knowledge would come to me so gradually that it was not so vivid and clear to me. It was like the seed of a tree, I was aware of the growth but not sure how it was happening. The misdeeds of the flesh were dying as I was waking up to the Spirit of God, as hi light continued to grow within me my soul realized its own path began to approach the journey of life from a spiritual understanding as I was trying to figure things and get answers to my 'why?' My major concern was why I was given this type of a body when I was fully aware from inside that I am fully capable of things I was failing to do on my own.

The power of awareness is those questions we always avoid or we are not allowed to ask. Ask them and you shall receive answers.

Personal Reflection Exercise

a) Find a quiet place and sit comfortably.

b) Close your eyes. Take a deep breath in and slowly breathe out, feel your body relax. Do it at least 3 times.

c) Now that you are aware of true life in you, with your eyes closed, feel your being from the top of your head down to your toes. Breathing is life, therefore take a deep breath from the deep chest and release it slowly from the top to bottom of your being. This will help you to rejuvenate the flow of life from your inner being to your physical body. You are establishing your connection to the Source of life, collecting your blessings from the inner man in order to influence your body to submit to your potential and purpose of your life. As you relax, allow your mind to receive, let it explore your world and uncover the unknown for you. Don't try to understand anything for now, just be free and let life flow. Don't control your mind by trying to think a thought or make sense out of anything, or judge anything. Let go and let God lead your spirit. Your spirit knows that He is God.

d) Say your prayers. And slowly bring back your senses to your breath and slowly open your eyes.

Chapter 3
The Journey of Overcoming and Becoming

"I have said these things to you, that in me you may have peace. In the world you will have tribulations, but fear not, take heart, I have overcome the world." John 16:33

We all have the physical bodies, in these bodies we have organs, we have blood flowing and we all breathe in and out, all these are physical components working closely together to make sure life (body and soul) is preserved as long as the physical body can live. But whilst we have the same components that are expected to work and function in the same manner, like we know that legs are for mobility, eyes are for sight and ears are for hearing, we differ in our functioning, we see differently, we walk differently and we perceive and discern differently. We approach life from different angles of perspective and have different purposes and destinies. Like birds flying in the air, it is like some are coming whilst others are going, at the same time it feels like we are heading towards the same direction.

Life feels like we are coming from somewhere going somewhere and we then stop by for an hour or so for a moment of fun and adventure before we proceed with our journey. For a little while, we put on some work clothes, protective clothes good enough to make sure we do not mess ourselves whilst we play with dirt and have fun. We take out all the tools and stuff, gadgets and everything that will make this moment of fun worthwhile, we then enjoy and experience fun, taking each minute at a time while it lasts. Time will come for us to pack up and move on with the journey. That 'stop by' moment in time and space is what we are calling life, the physical life is when we put on the physical body and we start going out and about living life.

The world is the place of adventure and a playground or we can say it is an amusement park where we take time to showcase endless possibilities of life within us, where the power that creates worlds manifests its creative abilities into being or takes form. It is a wonderful world of adventure where we come on stage and play out our inner world which reveals the life flowing from the Source. The world itself is there to present to us circumstances that can help us to unlock the power within and see how best we can rise above these circumstances and conquer the limitations of the physical world. There are endless challenges and tribulations around the world which require supernatural powers to come through and help us overcome them. Our physical body Is given the capacity to draw out this power from within and look at circumstances from a supernatural power side of view whereby you accept the challenge, we say nothing is impossible with God and He who is in us is greater than the one in the world, He will surely show up through you to provide a the solution in times of need. Life is an adventure.

But how are we living this big adventure?

One of the biggest question in life for everyone is what is the purpose of life? The general answer we get most of the time is life is for personal growth and development or attainment, to grow and become successful. The process of personal growth and development comprises of overcoming experiences or realities and becoming our potential over and over again, transcending to our higher selves as we continue traversing this world of endless possibilities pursuing our own unique expressions and experiences. This physical life can be a moment of adventure where we experience life from its other side, the manifestation reality of the non-physical energies. We come here to define who or what we are in the non-physical, therefore we manifest our unlimited being to showcase our unique expressions and potential. Accumulation of wealth and prosperity, to a certain extent, does not necessarily mean we have succeeded in life, you could have just discovered some techniques on the subject of that helps you accumulate wealth.

Being aware or becoming familiar with these realities helps us to continue to unveil the unknown realities from time to time removing the shells from our eyes of understanding so that we see things better every time. It is all about finding your place and discover the secrets. We always think we are all pursuing same stuff, money, love, happiness and all that, Very true, we all want that, but if it was only that then why should we pursue, why not just feel happy and get done with it and move on? Why not just move on the moment we get a few dollars? Why do we keep wanting more from life? Satisfaction. We want satisfaction in all things!

We need to understand that the need for satisfaction is not coming from the physical body but from inside where the inner man knows the fullness of life that truly satisfies the whole being, it is the spiritual being crying out for that eternal satisfaction from inside, he who drinks from this well will never thirst again. So we need to give attention to the one inside, to be mindful of the things that pertain to the higher self, awakening the real man who came down to this world to dwell in you, so that he can fully participate in living the life that can satisfy him.

Therefore, personal development and spiritual growth is having an ability to align the physical body to the spiritual body in order to understand the purpose of life and how to achieve it. It is the dialogue between the two entities so that they reach a mutual understanding of what needs to be done in this life, finding out what is on the other side of the other so that we gather all the components required from both worlds in order to collectively work together for the soul to realize and achieve its mission.

Awareness begins with thoughts that come to the mind, thoughts are normally brought in from outside by the sensory system, what we see, hear, taste, touch and smell is what starts the mind conversation. Also sometimes when we are relaxed and free, thoughts just come through and we start going deeper into conversations with ourselves. We start having questions around a particular subject. These questions we ask from within will always lead us to knowledge and knowledge is a precursor to experience and the more we deliberately ask questions, is the more we come into better understanding, we eventually experience and manifest what we know.

My favorite verse in the bible says "For God so loved the that He gave his only begotten son that whosoever believeth in him shall not perish but have eternal life", underline 'believeth'. This verse shows how deep the love of God is to mankind because, after all the historical works and everything we know about God, all he wants from us is to just believe in the Son, nothing more nothing less. On the other hand, its simplicity implies how complicated the Son is for us to believe and attain the eternal life, things should not be that easy and simple like that.

God wants us to know but believing is the starting point. Believing is a lower degree of knowing along the journey towards knowledge. You do not have to believe what you already know for knowing can be evidenced by a proved experience of what you already know, it has now reached a point beyond reasonable doubt, so you now do not only believe it but you also know it.

Belief is made up of constant thoughts, or a sequence of thoughts that keep coming to your mind, those thoughts will eventually grow and mature into a belief and then knowledge as you continue to experiment and experience the reality of these thoughts, closing the gap between belief and knowledge. Therefore, contextually, believing is a lower level of consciousness where you are just aware that the Son came from God, just a mere thought around that subject. But what if we decide to dive deeper and take a journey towards knowledge knowing more about things concerning this Son? We can only imagine what happens if we then come to the full knowledge, understanding his life and purpose, his ministry and all that he accomplished? It can be heaven on earth, we will automatically enter into the Kingdom of God without any restrictions because you surpassed the terms and conditions set by going beyond believing, you are fully established in the knowledge of the Son and you can have access to the eternal life.

As much as God wants his knowledge to abound in us, he says belief is sufficient enough for us to have access to eternal life. This is how deep knowledge is, there is power in knowing and there is more power in applying the knowledge you acquire as you pursue it. Just believing that you are carrying your soul inside your physical body, can just be enough to access your inner world and uncover what lies beneath, all the hidden treasures that eagerly wait for you to discover and be revealed to the world out there.

Being aware of yourself and environment inside and outside of your life helps you to identify and define who you are and how you present or express your persona to the world. You are able to understand your unique purpose as an individual and define your place in the collective consciousness in the bigger picture of the universal plan.

Not being aware does not empower us to move consciously, it takes away the joy of life, it is like moving in the dark, you are all over the place trying to guess the right way to go. We remain limited and get addicted to thoughts and habits we already know that are happening around us. This deprives us the joy of adventure, the joy of discovering endless possibilities available for us, the joy of finding our potential, the joy of launching the rockets of desires coming from inside, the joy to take a journey from the heart to the mind and face the truth about ourselves. The joy of overcoming our limitations and becoming our own superman.

Fear of the unknown is one of the greatest fears in life that stops us from pursuing our potential. We are afraid of what lies beyond what we do not know, we rather remain with what we already have experienced than step into the unknown so that we level up to a new experience, we feel safe and content, so comfortable in the past experiences we have lived than in the future experiences yet to be discovered. Yet life is summed up with experiences, it is a collection of what you have experienced in all aspects of life and how you have lived within the capacity of your potential.

The capacity is the measurement of volume of your energy that you use to reach your fullest potential and the energy comes in levels of quality. Lower level is when we are not able to function from a place that empowers us to perform our best, while higher level of energy is when we are performing beyond our abilities and limitations, doing the impossible. So awareness helps you to navigate our path, collect and harness the good quality of energy so that you are able to build a good quality lifestyle which is aligned from the inside to outside.

It is very possible to live a fulfilled life inside out, but it all depends on your level of consciousness or quality of energy you carry. It starts from the inner world then manifests on the surface, like the words we pray in the Lord's prayer, "Thy kingdom come on earth as it is in heaven", the heaven is the inner world that has it all and is anxiously waiting to deliver the kingdom treasures on earth just as it is in heaven.

All it takes is for you to unlock that door to the inner world, enter into your heaven and have conversations with your inner depths, look in the inside and search for the unknown for there lies the endless possibilities that you are yet to discover. Yes you carry that heaven and you are not even aware of it, you reside and walk around with it and yet you are looking for it out there. You are the best solution to all your problems and challenges, consult yourself first and it is possible that your solution can manifest from someone or somewhere else but the energy to manifest it comes from inside you then it attracts the possible solutions from the outside world. The world contains everything you need, there is no way in the world you would desire things that you have never seen before somewhere, the fact that you can conceive it in your mind, you can imagine and see it, means that it exists and it is possible to manifest it.

Let's talk about levels of energy. I have a physical disability, the condition is called Cerebral Palsy, and both my parents are gone, my siblings are out of Zimbabwe with their own families, left the country due to economic hardships we are currently facing in our country. Literally, on the physical side, things appear not to be okay, I should be the loneliest and miserable poor little thing alive.

There are times I allow myself to get so depressed that I feel suicidal, just want to die and forget that I ever existed. Then at times I miss my mother that I can cry in grief for hours that you would think she died yesterday. Also those times I just feel that my disability is just unbearable and sad that its stands as a barrier in my life, I would throw a pity party and cry in misery. Despite this cracky side, I also have those epic moments when I am just over the moon thinking and feeling so proud of myself, amazed that I am a good digital marketer, web designer and a lifestyle blogger, now an author. This really excites me and I feel so good about myself. There are moments I get excited knowing that my brother and sister are out of the country and think about the money and all the goodies they send me, the dreams of good life when my sister finishes her studies, the long distance calls with her and kids, oh you can imagine how happy and super excited I get. Even when I call my brother's daughters, I feel so loved and close to my family. Those are magical moments. Did you notice the variance in level of energy between high and low frequency?

That's how life is, the frequency of the energy is generated from inside, how you feel and think is what creates your life. That is why it is said you are the creator of your own destiny, you become what you think and feel, thoughts are the language of the mind to your brain and feelings are the language used to communicate to your body. How do I become the creator? By thinking. In my case, my day starts with a thought that I allow to come into my mind, remember thoughts are formed on the quality of energy. Lower energy attracts negative thoughts and higher energy attracts positive thoughts. Therefore, thoughts are just free travelers on your mind but it is up to you to reflect and regulate what stays and what leaves, it is all up to you to choose what to entertain and what to dismiss.

When a thought comes to mind, the mind sends signals to the brain to take action depending on what is on the mind, the brain is the physical side of the mind, and it is the brain that communicates to the mind the functions of the body, it detects the emotions and feelings, and sends signals to the body and the body reacts depending on the quality of emotion received.

It is natural to react, we respond to what we receive emotionally depending on the message or thoughts communicated, happy or sad, excited or scared, love or hate, all these emotions are triggered by thoughts depending on the level of energy that carried them through. The problem is not in the thought, it is in the processing of the thought where it has to determine the reaction and emotion and also how long we can maintain that state of emotion until it changes into another energy frequency by allowing another thought. For example, when I think of my disability, depending on which wave the energy is flowing on, it is either I entertain it because it is giving me good vibes, like I am seeing myself as an inspiration to others because I am defying all odds by pursuing my dreams, therefore, I entertain the thought and expand on it as I think more on how to keep inspiring others. I can dismiss the thought when my disability is making me feel sad, miserable and lonely, thinking of my physical limitations.

The mind is a world of choices and decisions, if we think deliberately, fully aware of what comes into mind and watch over our thoughts, then we wouldn't have to spend a day being miserable over things that we cannot change, we would choose to live happily ever after for the rest of our lives by allowing thoughts that makes us feel good about ourselves all the time and dismissing thoughts that deny us joy and happiness.

That is what I call true joy, joy of overcoming our limiting beliefs and becoming our true by seeing what serves us and holding onto it while letting go of what doesn't, now that is growth. We overcome by allowing our minds to be aware of the thoughts that come through and regulate them, take time to consciously consider what stays for expansion and what we can let go. Being conscious of our thoughts from time to time, our minds will eventually get the constant point of attraction and know what to accept or decline. Practice makes perfect, our thoughts will turn into habits which will later become our lifestyles and the character which we are becoming.

This is a journey of fine-tuning, we see things and realize your need for satisfaction in them, if they do not satisfy emotionally, we turn from them to look at the other side of the emotion and consider closing the gap in between.

This requires us to be aware of what kind of thoughts our energy is capable of generating. We need to develop a third eye that has the ability to monitor the mind. When a thought enters the mind, we hold and rise above it so that we are able to see what is on the other side of the thought, both front and back views. For instance, if you think of making a call and you are procrastinating, maybe you want to call your mother, you should rise above that thought and consider the joy of hearing her voice and the happiness of knowing she is fine. By just processing that thinking , you already feel excited and happy as if you have already made that call, it generates the signal to the brain and tells it to be happy, it asks why and it is told, because mummy loves my calls and that makes me happy, the brain then communicates the emotion to the body and you become excited and you grab your phone to call mummy. Now you actualize the thought and turn thoughts into things. If we think a thought and dwell on it negatively or carelessly, it manifests exactly that, what we feed into our minds is what we become.

The funny thing we do not know about our human body is that we are not aware that our brain does not know the difference between the past and the future, therefore it generates exact emotions from the past or future in real-time, like I can feel the pain of the death of my mother any time and cry as if it has just happened, it is replayed in the mind and it causes same pain as it happened in the past the day she died as I think and talk about it. The brain on its own does not know it is playing an old tape. The brain is not the mind, it does not have the ability to discern, we will need to communicate to the brain that there is no need to play that tape from the past, do not waste your time and energy on that. How about creating a new tape of mummy enjoying and having fun on the other side of life. With that thought, using imagination, the mind will pull out a tape from nowhere and I will watch my mummy smiling from heaven over us and being proud of her children.

That is how we overcome the negative thoughts no matter how strong the influence coming from outside, the power lies in the mind. The mind can influence our whole life just the way it influence our mood of the day. Like I said before, it is ok to react or to feel sad, miserable, poor, unworthy, self-doubt, just as it is ok to feel good, happy, worthy, loved, encouraged, wealthy, but the earliest we become aware of the quality of energy we are feeling, the better, being aware helps us to regulate and replace the emotion with the one that empowers us before another wrong one comes in again and again and build a software program which the brain will be using for the rest of your life, becoming our daily bread.

The moment of glory is when we awaken to the reality of the matter, the realization that this kind of thought is not aligned to what we want to achieve, this kind of thinking does not promote me to greater heights, it does not help me create good feeling in me, it does not give me the energy required to take action towards my purpose.

WHAT IS ON THE OTHER SIDE

That moment is capable of taking us to higher places, instantaneous rate of of manifestation that will help us grow and reach our potential. So imagine if those moments become our way of life, experimenting and playing around with this kind of power and ability, we will experience transfiguration everyday.

Manifestation of our thoughts, turning thoughts into things, is so magical that when we master the art we become beyond unstoppable when all sides of realities are in alignment, both worlds facing each other. Our physical bodies now understand and submit to our inner man and let him take charge and influence the adventure of life. As much as things we want to have or achieve become clear and vivid, at times manifestation is not as instant as we want it to be. I have realized that the joy is not really in the destination, it is in the journey to destiny, the space between getting there is what gives satisfaction.

The 'becoming' is when we are gathering resources available for manifestation, defining and identifying the components, gathering things from inside and launching the rockets of desires inspired by thoughts and feelings, developing abilities and skills that will be required as tools and equipment that will be used to manifest the visions, passions and dreams into realities. The world and environment around us will present to us situations and circumstances to compare and contrast so that we can make choices, and identify our preferences, all these will inspire us to have desires. We can meet someone driving a nice car and we smile at the thought of driving our own car too as nice as that one, the desire is launched and how to will manifest it depends on the thoughts and energy coming together to take action to get this car. This car is not going to fall from the sky, money should be available in the bank to buy it, or a well wisher should locate you and feel the urge to call and give you that car, or a lottery program somewhere should identify the number on your ticket you bought so that you become a winner and you buy that car with the money.

Whatever way, the magic is in the fine details of the manifestation, realizing how things come into being, is like God taking his time molding and fashioning us in his own image and likeness. That process is what makes creation special, everything else was called forth out of nowhere and appeared instantly, but the man was put together detail by detail by the Creator himself, he breathe life into being. The real joy is putting details in the process The details in-between are what we are here to experience as spiritual beings in the human body because everything else is very possible in the spirit life for there is no partiality, there are no blurry lines in the spirit, we see things as they are, there is no comparing and contrasting. We are here as an extension of the non-physical power on a mission to experience its own power on a personal level of consciousness. Everything is available and possible but it needs to be accessed from the deep.

What is stopping you from being happy then if all is inside? Is it easier said than done?

Life Experience

I think I gave too much of my life experience in the previous chapter which is very relevant to this chapter as well. So I won't take too of my time on this one.

As I became aware of life more and more, I came to some conclusions that helped me to embrace myself and understand how life was going. Despite the circumstances and anxieties I faced, there is somehow a deep understanding inside that always reassures me to keep going. I am not saying I am fully convinced beyond reasonable doubt about life, I still struggle with everything just like everyone else, but after self-doubt and feeling unworthy because of circumstances, I still feel the inner man in the temple reading to me the good Word of encouragement and support, I feel I can still go beyond the challenges and overcome them all one by one, as I keep reaching out for more, I am believe there are endless possibilities available in the universe.

WHAT IS ON THE OTHER SIDE

Manifestation is what I will become in the end of it all, it is on the other side of the journey which gives me faith that one day I will get there. Faith is about things hoped for as we anticipate to manifest them. But there is a journey I am traveling going there. I am busy filling in the details of who I am becoming by facing each and every challenge, choose from contrasting situations provided. All I need is to be wise as choose what serves my purpose from what doesn't.

I am a disabled, orphaned, single, lonely poor old girl living in an economically devastating country, I am also that intelligent miss independent sitting pretty in a wheelchair who always gets attention wherever she goes because I am just too beautiful not to be noticed. I am fully aware of the current situation but I am always looking for what could be found on the other side, always anticipating the best side of things

For me, there is joy in solving my challenges everyday, I call it counting wins of the day. Jesus talked about loving our enemies, in Mathew 5:46, he said, "For if you love those loving you, what reward do you have?" Enemies are not always people but even things in your life working against your purpose. By identifying my abilities and limitations, I am also identifying my friends and enemies,, my loved ones are them that are strong and helping me on my way to my destiny whilst enemies are the physical limbs that are weak and not aligned to serve my purpose, I will need to embrace them, love and support them as I negotiate with them so I can close the gap between weak and strong as the whole system works together towards fulfilling my purpose. If I fail to work on my weaknesses , physically, emotionally, intellectually and spiritually, then ho do I achieve my goals and how will I grow? Growth is when you see weaknesses as destiny helpers and that propels you towards progress. My truest joy, as far as my disability is concerned, is when I find a solution to achieving a certain task on my own no matter how small it is, I celebrate every inability that I overcome everyday.

There is joy in overcoming limitations for that is part of the journey towards becoming our true unique self. Manifestation is when the whole of me is called out to come forth to be revealed for everyone to now see the truest expression of God in me. The joy that we experience along the journey in small achievements is what builds up the eternal satisfaction which is waiting for us in the future. Rejoice always again I say rejoice, for that joy will be redeemable on the other side.

Personal Reflection Exercise

a) Find a quiet place and sit comfortably.

b) Close your eyes. Take a deep breath in and slowly breathe out, feel your body relax. Do it at least 3 times.

c) With your eyes closed, do the exercises in the end of Chapter 1 and 2.

d) Once you enter the inner temple, remember your body is the temple of God, you will now know who you are in Christ. He will open the eyes of spiritual understanding so that you see things from a spiritual point of view, blessed are the pure in heart for they shall see God. As you receive from the spirit of God, you will see things from a higher perspective. After seeing God, your mind will be transformed into the mind of God to enable you to discern things as they are all and define what serves your purpose from what doesn't. You acknowledge your current situation and define what needs to be changed for the better, where you are and where you want to be. Then your spirit will have receive ideas on how to close this gap. As you go out and about during your day, practice the art of listening to yourself so that you can receive impulses and intuitions of what you downloaded into your spirit. Trust the process, you will be guided throughout your day.

e) Say your prayers. And slowly bring back your senses to your breath and slowly open your eyes

MOLLEN GARIKAI

Chapter 4
The Present Moment

".... but those who live according to the Spirit set their minds on the things of the Spirit. For to set the mind on the flesh is death, but to set the mind on the Spirit is life and peace." Romans 8:5-6

It is our primary responsibility to regulate our thoughts in order to have a healthy mind and emotionally balanced state. Responsibility simply means the ability to respond, meaning we all have the capacity to respond to a situation depending on what we are aware of concerning the subject we are responding to, at times the response comes up automatically, like we do not need to think twice when a hand accidentally touches the hot plate, that moment is to scream and remove the hand and run around the house to survive the moment. We are responding to the pain that came from outside but the energy or reactional impulses to survive is coming from inside. The energy is always available for emergency moments like these, they are reflex actions and impulses responding to sensory receptors and nervous system. This is physical body system energy. But responding or reacting to thoughts and circumstances is a different situation because we can choose to give ourselves time to become aware of the thought and give it attention, we can consider to take action upon it or not. This also needs energy for emotional purpose depending on the alternatives at hand, for instance, generally loving the thought of calling your mother, you can get excited about it and you can also be calm about it, you might need extra energy if you want to tell her super exciting news.

High emotional energy flows from our higher-self to support our well-being, to increase our value and give us good empowering emotions, while low energy is the enemy of progress, it demotivates, discourages and separates us from our higher-self. There is nothing wrong in reacting to thoughts however way we feel, positive or negative, what makes it wrong is when the feeling does not feel good. The amount of time we remain in that state of emotion of not feeling good is what kills. Why do we spend our valuable energy generating emotions that do not support our well-being?

Energy is generated in the mind, our level of consciousness and awakening, what we think and believe is what builds our energy field and that energy is what creates our constant thought pattern which enables us to pursue knowledge as we grow from perspective to higher perspectives. The higher and wider our energy keeps expanding, the better we become in the mastering the game of aligning our body, mind and soul to the Source of life.

It is said that one has to change and think differently in order to see change in the outside world. Having the same thoughts everyday will not change our circumstance or situation. When I am not happy about something, I sit up straight, take a deep breath and start rearranging my mind, monitor my mind to see how I can do things differently in order to change the matter for me to feel good. Lets try to be greater than our environment and find that point of elevation where we are able to see and imagine what is on the other side of the situation. We can actually create a feeling of what we want to change and get the chance to experience it in the mind before we experience it in the body or in reality.

We have two sources of emotions and these are love and fear. Love is when our mind is connected to the higher-self that resides and functions from a higher point of elevation and where we experience the emotions that support our well-being in every aspect of our lives and aims to fulfill our purposes and destinies. This is a place of love, happiness, peace, joy, acceptance, fulfillment, unlimited possibilities, creativities, awakening, endless knowledge, place of understanding and enlightenment, place of remembering and becoming one with the universe. On the other hand, fear is a place of separation, rebellion, resentment, depression, stress, bitterness, judgmental, anger, hatred, place of lack, scarcity and shame, ignorance and darkness, place of dull and dim moments where nothing grows, no hope and expectations. It is a place where you can not create anything, that place is an emergency ward where you can die and forget about life, you suffocate and die due to lack of energy.

Let's talk about fear, no one wants to live in fear but we always find ourselves scared of things and situations, the dangers in life that we think might happen to us, unwanted but expected outcomes, loss and even things we don't know yet can consume us with fear. When we don't see the evidence of assurance that everything is fine, we lose trust and hope, we then get scared of the predicted circumstances. When we lose hope, the next thing is fear. Fear is the absence of love, where there is love there is no fear at all because love does not err, everything is perfect therefore there isq assurance and certainty that everything is going well no matter the situation we are facing. FEAR is an illusion, False Events Appearing Real.

There are real scary events happening in real life and the body has the ability to generate enough energy required to survive such events, the body is always ready to protect and fight against any danger at any moment, it is always sensitive to any signal of danger it picks from its surroundings and, like an animal, it is always ready to attack in order to survive. There are some fears we have that are more on the intellectual level than on the physical body, fear of rejection, for example, thinking of death, loss, poverty, lack, failure, betrayal, guilt, shame, divorce, people's opinions, fear of the unknown and all that we fear secretly from within. These kinds of fears are coming based on past experiences, what we already know and can predict the outcome, they come from what we feed the mind.

When a thought enters the mind it is there for attention, negative or positive, what we give attention always leads to manifestation and the more we linger on it is the more it becomes a known resident of the mind and makes itself comfortable. Thoughts are influenced by our environment, daily living, surroundings, people in our lives, careers, beliefs and so on. The mind is a very busy industrial site where billions of thoughts are always coming through, we can only stop thinking when we go down to sleep but even in sleep mode I think the mind does not totally shutdown. Thoughts are normally initiated from memories or from the expected future. Memories are a collection of recorded images of past experiences and imaginations are a collection of recorded images of expected future.

There is a space in-between the past and the future which we will call the Now-Moment, the present moment has no need to record because It is an active continuous state of flow from past to future. It is a moment of knowing the unknown, a moment of creating new realities, and of free will to determine the next experience. It is a time of stillness whereby we are neither here nor there, neither in the past nor future, we are not defined by any experience we know or known based on space and time, nobody are nobody nowhere in the vast of the continuous state of life, we are one with everything else. We are with God in the stillness of the now. Be still and know that I am God.

Having established my understanding of fear and the state of the mind, let's now look into the other state of emotion which is love. Love is indeed a beautiful thing, they say, he who finds love finds life. This is a place of wholeness, connection, abundance, limitless, fulfillment, enlightenment, realization, gratitude and so on. These are elevated emotions that are found in the absence of fear. When the body senses danger whilst we are in an emotional state of love, there are higher chances of surviving the situation because there is enough energy generated by these emotions, enough support from within the system itself, there is no need to turn up the turbines to generate enough energy to deal with the situation.

Calmness and stillness is very possible when you feel the abundance of love and life, limitless, endless possibilities, hope, faith, supported, encouraged and positive. When the mind is being influenced or informed by such emotions then its ability to transcend beyond the situation in that moment becomes greater than the circumstances. We are able to watch the situation from a higher point and have a full view of what is going on in the situation we are facing in that moment with no strings attached that can we can not judge based on what we know from the past or predict the outcome. There will be a steady flow of endless possibilities for that situation in love and in gratitude. From this height of energy we are able to create anything, nothing is impossible and nothing matters. In the unknown world is where we are able to attract support from the universe to work out our purposes in life.

To sum up this insight, the magical moment in life is not in the past which is already gone, nor in the future which is yet to come, but in the Now-Moment where we neither know nor not. In actual fact, know the unknown, we are there when things are happening in their truest reality. We are watching events from the higher perspective in order to choose, out of the possibilities made available, the best that serves our well-being at every level of our life. As much as there is a lot going on in life, knowing that it is us who create our world and reality, there is no need to fear or wait for the future to happen when it is us who decide on the emotions that we want to feel.

Faith is also the opposite of fear, the bible says, "Faith is the substance of things hoped for, the evidence of things not seen", therefore, when we are above our environment, our vision and desire is very clear and vivid on what we want, then we are on top of the world. Faith is the capacity of high level energy available for us in the invisible world where anything is possible, everything is good and perfect.

In the unknown or invisible world we are powerful and in charge of our destiny, we don't wait for outside forces to create happiness for us because we will be screening and removing what we don't want from our mind for our own good. If happiness and joy is what we want, then be happy and enjoy that instance.

What if we deliberately and continuously choose to rejoice always, a sequence of joyful instances moment after moment. There is power in standing by the gate of our mind making sure that it is not every Jack and Jill that knocks on the gate and gets the privilege to enter through it and roam around freely, trust me, the moment we realize this we will never leave the gate open, that is the only time in our entire life we will accept gatekeeping as our lifetime career.

Personal Reflection Exercise

a) Find a quiet place and sit comfortably.

b) Close your eyes. Take a deep breath in and slowly breathe out, feel your body relax. Do it at least 3 times.

c) With your eyes closed, do the exercises in the end of Chapter 1 and 2.

d) Quietly remember that you are in the throne of God, In the stillness of the moment is where God come to meet you, like he to Elijah. Hold on to this moment as he makes the impossible possible for you. Walk on the waters like Peter, your eyes on God and no questions. This is not the time to ask why and how but what more can you get from God. Put your trust God Almighty who creates worlds in the whole universe, he will surely open windows of heaven for you and pour his lifetime blessings for you.

e) Say your prayers. And slowly bring back your senses to your breath and slowly open your eyes

Chapter 5
What is On The Other Side

"In him was life, and the life was the light of men. The light shines in the darkness, and the darkness has not overcame it." John 1:5

On the other side of fear there is love. Fear is the expression of separation and discord, anger, anxiety, sadness, discouraged, guilty, unworthy,, all negative emotions come from the in depth feeling of separation. Fear is the mother of all negative emotions.

God is life and he is the Source of all life. The story of the fallen angels helps me understand, to a certain extent, the context of separation and discord between the non-physical and physical worlds. Let me share with you my reflection on the story of the fallen angels. Please hear me out, this is just my own version of contemplation (not a doctrine, not found anywhere in the scripture). This is me thinking things out.

In the beginning of life, way before the physical world, God, the Supreme non-physical being, the Universe, Holy Spirit, the Divine who is Life, was just there doing life alone, experiencing life in its truest essence and with all the energies, Mighty wonders, powers and glory. All life was and still is in Him fully and completely, all knowledge and capabilities, He is the fullness of life, he is Life living in Life in everything, he is the whole complete picture of life. This Life is what we call the Divine Spirit, the bible says, the Spirit hovered above the waters. This life was there for the longest time in the eternity beyond our time and space in the past, present and future. My understanding tells me that the Spirit is the body of non-physical energies that creates worlds and everything found in life, it is the self-contained power that makes life happen. Everything is made by Him, in Him, through Him and for Him, to demonstrate His Mighty power and glory. Nothing exists outside this Spirit Life.

Just like the electricity current is a supply of power with wide range of different capabilities and functions only realized by what it is operating on, its volume and capacity or voltage distribution is what actualizes the power and its function, it has the power to light up the whole country at once as well as to just turn on a small radio somewhere. It depends on the functions, but it is available for everything connected and aligned for it to flow and make things happen, it is the same energy we use to cook, to watch TV, to use the computer, to drill a borehole, to operate an industrial machine, and so on, but the energy is distributed accordingly. So it is with the Spirit, the Non-physical energy is the creative energy that gives life to the whole universe of existence.

Spirit Life was lived in the vastness and sameness of everything, hovering above the waters, (maybe I will see if I can also talk about the waters later), but let me just say the waters are the components used by the non-physical in the physical world, calling forth things into existence, this, creation and manifestation. Creativity can be understood as the activity of turning this energy into things, or allowing the energy flow to be distributed according to the potential and endless possibilities that the energy can be translated into being. By sameness, I mean there is no contrast, no opposition of things, there is holy communion – common union of the Divine life, all is at one with the Divine, everything is real and clear, no blurred lines or discord.

So how did contrast and opposition come in? Here is how it is being unveiled to me. The story of Lucifer and the fallen Angels brought me closer to another place of understanding as it helps me to go beyond the creation story in Genesis. There is nowhere in the bible where this story is fully narrated, but the Christian theologies show that the sins of the fallen angels took place before the beginning of the human life, being led by Lucifer in the rebellion against God. The book of Revelations in chapter 12 tells us about Satan the deceiver of the whole world, being defeated in the war in heaven and being thrown down to earth together with a third of angels out of heaven.

I am not going to get so much into deep biblical context on what caused war in heaven, remember this is just a personal reflection journey towards full understanding my identity and place in this life.

God lived alone for eternity in his own presence, creating worlds in the universe, his creative abilities were mighty and powerful. Behold it was good. But it was all in Himself, for Himself alone, by Himself. At some point in life He desired to evolve and expand. He wanted more out of himself. In Genesis 2.18 says, 'And the Lord said, "It is not good that the man should be alone, I will make him a helper."' God had had that experience too, he lived alone in the vastness of the universe and he wanted a helper. In all his entire work of creation, I think the best and special moment ever was when He decided to bring forth another entity like himself, giving life to another being who became his soulmate and his helper to live with. The new being was created in the likeness of the creator, possessing everything that was of God, mighty powers, all abilities and glory. I believe God desired so much to see his own glory, revealed and experienced in another entity, he wanted to watch Himself from outside Himself. I would like to think Lucifer was the bone of God's bones, flesh of his flesh as he was taken out of God. He was named Lucifer, Luci means Light and -feri means carry or bearer, God is the Light, Lucifer was the bearer of Light so he was given the life of God to bear it .

These two souls lived together for a very long time, living their best lives, fully connected to one another in love and harmony, fully aware of the their unique identities and realities of this divine union. This was the beginning of relativity, the Spirit being was now in a relationship with someone where he had to define, identify and distinguish things, in contrast of others. Contrast brings forth clarity, we wouldn't know a female if there was no male, you would not know what is good if there is nothing to compare it to. In this case, we see God the Father, the Creator, the Giver, whilst the other one is God the Son, the Begotten or created, the Receiver, the other side of God, for Him to be called Father he gave birth to a son. There is a relationship going on here.

The Spirit of God is the giver of life which makes him the Supreme Power above everything. The definition of the word 'real' or 'truth' is something that can never be changed, this reality of God is immovable, he is not able to shift his position for he is Life itself. Supremacy belongs to Him God the Father.

They lived together fully convinced that God is the Ultimate Source of everything in the universe, and Lucifer on the other hand, being the first on the scene to experience life with him, was the Ultimate Receiver of everything in the universe as well, including all mighty powers, abilities and wisdom, he was the heir-apparent. To allow the natural flow of energy, the Giver needed the Receiver, the Father loved the Son. They were on the extreme end of the other, God being the first to give and Lucifer, on the other hand, the first to receive life God. .

Love was their ultimate energy that constantly kept flowing to them, keeping them together and developing their creative abilities and capabilities for the purpose of continuity of life, expansion, immortality, eternity and beyond. They would always look at each other as extension or expansion of the other, the magnificence of one would reflect in another. No one was better than the other, one was different from the other in the uniqueness of individuality of their being. They were not duplicated copies of beings but original identities with same features but different functions that enabled them to function differently with same capacity and capabilities to achieve common goals, for instance, the ability to receive is different from the ability to give. This was the life in the Spirit.

Love is the flow of life, power and energy from God in constant supply to create endlessly. Being aware of love and the source of this eternal power in its abundance is a perfect place to be, being aware of abundance, endless or limitless is what gives relief or freedom to claim anything in the universe, the recipient can live a life of pointing things, putting them in a wish list or basket and wait for delivery, no need to be anxious on how and when they will arrive because you know the storehouse is forever full and it is a matter of requesting for what you want and it is given to you. That was the situation then, the two aware in abundance of love and life, the other one was the giver of light whilst the other was the light bearer, we will talk about light some other time but light represents knowledge, therefore, God was the giver of knowledge, the revelator, whilst Lucifer was the bearer of knowledge, his job was to remain in the presence of light for clarity about life, to understand the mysteries things happening in this life and know how to keep creating experience after experience as he continues to receive from the Source. The secret was in keeping the plug switched on and connected to the Source.

Fast forward...after a very long time, they created other spirit beings in their likeness and they too were given power and all abilities. They were their children having given them life, the two were parents of this Spirit family. The creation of life in that dimension went on for a long time without any discord or conflict, every spirit being was connected to the Father, the source of life, and was aware and committed to their purpose, fully functional and established in the wisdom and capacity of manifesting the glory of the kingdom. All were working out for the good of everyone without any external forces of influence for all were aware of their own truth and purpose, to live and serve God in perfect peace and harmony, to be co-creators, to be fruitful and multiply, to enjoy life and have fun, above all, to love themselves in one another.

The coming through of many others beings introduced the ability to co-exist and live together despite being created differently. That is relationship. Relativity was to allow diversity to exist in the sameness reality. Everything and everyone was so connected to the source that it was impossible to perform against the kingdom lifestyle even if they were free to do whatever they want because they were not even aware of anything except their common desire which to serve God and expansion of the universe. The free will was exercised for everyone's good. They were in the Light, in full knowledge of who they are and nothing was a mystery in the kingdom, they were not second-guessing or in doubt of their true identity and place in the universe, wisdom and knowledge was in abundance, knowing and was effortless.

Fast forward the story, the relationship between the God and Lucifer, the light and the light bearer, was an exclusive love affair, the epitome of love life in every other relationship that was yet to come. They were in love, like a father would love his, mother and child, husband and wife. Love is not love until it is shared or given away. Their life revolved around each other and everything was good and perfect.

The light bearer stayed connected always allowing the Light to flow and carrying it around wherever he went, the light was in him. God lived in him and he lived in God. The light resided in him to guide and reveal knowledge, it was available at any moment to give divine understanding and wisdom, to enlighten the kingdom with the power and the glory in order to make known the endless possibilities available to be explored and discovered. The light bearer would listen and learn from the Light within and understand the revealed knowledge, he was enlightened that he too may enlighten the kingdom and everyone else. He was the Light-house of God, the extension of the Light that the glory of Light was on him in fullness and in splendor that no one would understand the difference or the individuality of the Light and the bearer of Light.

The Light would reveal knowledge and the bearer would receive and realize it, as more light was asked for, it was given and received from the Source of Light, the more powerful, glorious, intelligent and brilliant the light bearer and the kingdom became. Functionality was the difference between them, the bearer was not the Light, the Light was not the bearer of Light, it was a relationship of the Source and the receiver. The bearer waited upon the Light to send and the Light waited upon the bearer to receive and bear the Light and the bearing was the understanding of the Light, uploading and downloading situation. There was cohesion of the two entities, they were in alignment and in sync.

That verse in the bible that says, 'Blessed is the one that gives than the one that takes,' points that both the giver and the receiver are great in their own way, it is a dependent relationship where one can not be there without the other, there is no giving when there is no receiving on the other end. But if it happens that the other chooses to disconnect from the other, if we contrast and compare, then the other becomes better than the other one, the difference becomes more distinguished than when they are together. In this case, the giver is more blessed than the one that that takes, Why? Because of content.

In digital we say content is king, the giver becomes superior because of the content and capacity or ability to give even though there is no way content can realize and manifest to itself, it cannot manifest what it already is. Content is that which is in motion, flowing and being transmitted from one end to another end, Unlike the receiver, the giver is full and whole on its own and lacks nothing but waits for a opportunity to manifest or express its desire. On the other hand, the receiver is empty and in lack on its own when separated from the giver. Therefore, receiver is the extension of the giver with the capability and capacity to receive and manifest but manifestation can only happen when content is received and realized. The receiver is inferior, empty and useless when it is disconnected from the source, but staying connected fills it with purpose and will to realize and actualize the glory of the Source. In manifestation, the power coming from the Source is revealed and shown to the external world through the receiver. It is an honest fact, that the receiver is inferior to the giver, content is king because it is the value coming from the Source to add to the recipient.

The Light is the revealer of all the knowledge there is to know, creation is when revealed knowledge is applied and transformed into something revealed in the knowledge. It brings visions of ideas and desires from the enlightened knowledge of Source into existence. It is Source finding his way into existence to experience manifestation.

I no longer have time to go further on about this relationship.

Let's just say there could be a moment in time when free will convinced Lucifer to disconnect from God or considered, out of curiosity, the idea of separation, what it could be like to be disconnected and live away from the Source. What is on the other side of where I am right now? This led to a reality where he was able to compare and contrast between the two factors, the giver and the receiver. Realizing the contrast, him being the Ultimate Receiver of everything and God being the Ultimate Giver, he fell into inferiority complex. He walked himself out of the comfort of his home, the Source of life, to find what was on the other side. He became the prodigal son.

Fear of losing the supply, insecurities or maybe he just wanted more than what he was getting, or he just wanted everything to himself, not to be at the receiving end, he wanted it all. Or maybe the process is what he wanted to do away with, the process of manifestation of his desires, he wanted to be where the desires are instantaneously fulfilled, he was no longer interested in the details in the flowing of things. So many possible reasons that caused this discord and it took place from a point of weakness or ignorance.

Disconnection from Light is the beginning of darkness, the two can never be in the same room at the same time, the entrance of light is the disappearance of darkness, no negotiations.

The bible says, people die because of lack of knowledge, darkness is the other side of Light which is knowledge, therefore, darkness is ignorance which leads to death whilst knowledge leads to life. Darkness conceived fear which is the mother of all the lower emotions such as pride, inferior, ego, desperation, unworthy, betrayal, emptiness, jealousy, resentment, anger, anxiety, lack , scarcity and hatred. These emotions can never bring anyone to that wonderful place of wholeness, connection, abundance, creativity. Lucifer became the Devil, the cursed one. He felt separated, lonely, not appreciated, unworthy and he could not perform or work in alignment with his purpose in the kingdom. The Light continued to dim its brightness as he went further and further away from God and he lacked the energy and ability to function or experience the Light in its full capacity. He was incapacitated that he failed to see things clearly and felt that he was the victim and it was an unfair predicament, yet nothing had changed, all he needed was to go back home and acknowledge his father, the source of life, tune in and turn on the switch to the giver of light which was always available for him, but he was blind in the dark.

It was not and still not possible to shift or move God from his position because, 'In the beginning God created...,' he is the beginning of everything and all belongs to Him including the one coming against him, everything is contained within himself even that drama of separation. He holds the whole wide world in his hands. We can only imagine the moment when God decides to shift his position a bit and stop everything, the whole existential system will completely shutdown and access to life won't be available even to the one who wants to take over.. God is that highest power in the universe, the deepest of depths, highest of all heights, and widest of all the widths in the universe. He cannot shift from that position even for a second, it is like a kettle asking to become electricity, that's impossible ! God is God and everything else are his subjects. Nothing can be done about it.

Separation happened and the light bearer felt empty and he actually went around in the kingdom conspiring with other spirits and influencing other subjects to help him feel how he was feeling and understand why he was feeling that way. The free will is a gift given to all and in the kingdom no one manipulates anyone to agree or disagree on anything, they are fully aware that every choice made comes with the ultimate effects. He reasoned together with other spirit beings who were not in alignment with the source, they genuinely sympathized with one another in their weakened state of emotion due to lack of knowledge and freely chose to emotionally support each other, or they resonated and the feeling was mutual, those who comforted him were actually feeling the same now that someone had decided to speak out , it now made more sense to themselves too.

So the kingdom was divided, it was now a compare and contrast reality show, a place of conflict and war, and as it continued, the separation gap grew bigger, the light can never be in the same house with darkness.

Disconnection took place, Light remained turned on but the bearer went away with the plug and darkness took him deeper and deeper into the woods of unknown ignorance. Nothing grows in darkness, the world of endless conflict and confusion, you don't expect anything to develop in a warzone where destruction and killings is the order of the day, it is not a place for wisdom and creativity, It is a state of survival and fear. Fear is the ultimate emotion which causes anger, hatred, resentment, and every other negative emotion.

Now on separation, what makes God remain on the wonderful and perfect side is that, there are laws that governs the kingdom and he is the giver and author of these laws, he also abides by them. These laws express his character, he is light, life and love. He can not kill or destroy because he is the giver of life, death can only be experienced in darkness, death is the separation from the Source of life.

The Light bearer rebelled against his source and became the other side of life, God is truth, Lucifer became the father of lies, nothing is true that comes from nowhere else except from the true source of life. The devil then became the source of all evil, fear, the dark, death and hatred. Whilst God gives life and light, the devil comes to kill and destroy, death and darkness belongs to him, he became the root of all evil.

All other subjects exercised their free will and fell from the throne of grace together with their father, the devil. From the beginning, he lied and deceived them to lure them to rebel against the kingdom. I don't think they were chased out of the kingdom, but they separated and isolated themselves, because they were blind, they were not able to have access to the source, they lost the sense of belonging to the extent that they were there, but due to fear and anger, shame and hatred, they were blind-folded and not aware of their true identity. They were now connected to the darkness.

God remained the giver life and all things that are good and perfect to them, but they needed to be connected for the continuous supply of life. Their new source that was now available was that of the evil one.

Take that narration as if I was just telling you one of the fairytales from ancient world where you just listen and digest. That is how I personally digested the story of the fallen angels, the great rebellion, not everyone fell but a certain percentage rebelled. The salvation story is for another day. So separation from the Source is what is called death, we die when we are separated from the giver of life.

Now that we see how the two forces work, they are on the extreme end of each other, we now understand what is on the other side of the other. As human beings we are an extension of both worlds with a free will to choose which side to be in alignment with. Knowledge is key that opens the door that leads into space of alignment with life and, on the other hand, ignorance is aligned to death.

The power and the glory await for those who are aligned to the Source of life and truth, it is readily available for those who pursue and seek to be filled in with the knowledge of truth. Jesus Christ said, 'I am the way, the truth and the life.' The way is the pursuing the things that leads you to the Source, things that trigger your mind to think of deeper things, things that create an environment and atmosphere to receive from the Source. The truth is the revealed knowledge from the Source, the spiritually enlightened understanding of this knowledge, seeing things from the Source's point of perspective. The Life is Source manifested in you, becoming the express knowledge of God, life is bearing the Light and possessing the power and the glory of God that dwells in us in abundance.

Personal Reflection Exercise

a) Find a quiet place and sit comfortably.

b) Close your eyes. Take a deep breath in and slowly breathe out, feel your body relax. Do it at least 3 times.

c) With your eyes closed, do the exercises in the end of Chapter 1 and 2.

d) With your eyes closed, remember you are have entered the temple, you are sitting before the throne of God and his garment fills the whole temple as it was described by Isaiah in chapter. Worship and praise him as you marvel at his glory, here is the place of power and glory where all your dreams and desires are conceived and created. Imagine yourself going before the alter, the Mercy Seat, kneeling down to worship and one of the angels comes to you with a candle and gives it to you. You are the of the world, no man puts a candle under a bed but on top for everyone to see the light. See yourself carrying that light as you move around this world. Let there be light in your world. Be enlightened on your path of life.

e) Say your prayers. And slowly bring back your mind and attention to your breath and slowly open your eyes

MOLLEN GARIKAI

Chapter 6

God is Love

"Beloved, if God so loved us, we ought to love one another. No one has ever seen God, if we love one another, God abides in us and his love is perfected in us.' 1 John 4:11-12

God is the life in our being, the Ultimate Source and giver of life, in him is all life we will ever know to serve our purpose of living. In the kingdom, the purpose of life is to love ourselves in one another. In the gospel of John, Jesus gave a new commandment that we love one another as he loved us. And I have a problem with the word 'commandments' whenever it is used in the context of the Divine. If God is to give a command as the highest office of the Commander In Chief of the whole universe, then it is no longer about choice and free will, we would just do what he says. So to me commandments in the bible sound more like commitments where we are urged to commit ourselves to follow the guidelines for things to work out for us, and it is contrast at play, choose between life and death. In this case, Jesus urges us to commit ourselves to love one another, which is to allow the life of God to through you as it continue to flow towards others.

One might ask, what is love? Let me try to express my own understanding on that.

As I have just mentioned, God is love and love is the life of God. Love is the highest power of God and his truest character, he who finds love finds God and the most beautiful expression of God. It is the highest level of consciousness where we can see God as he is. It is the place we find satisfaction when we are connected to the Source. Love lives in the enlightenment of knowledge that abounds in the purposes of life.

Love is the orgasm of life, that fullest ecstasy of the flow of energy of life that we feel when the heart is consumed by the fires of love. When I say, "I love you!", I'm saying, in between me (I) and 'you' there is (God) 'love', meaning when I look at you, I see the magnificence of God's truest and unique expression in you, you are that adapter that I plug intimately to feel and experience God in you. To a certain extent, love has not about sex because it is possible to have sex without love, rape is an act of sex without love, therefore, sex is not there to prove the presence of love. However, it is the deepest feeling of desire to be intimate with the something beyond the physical body. Sexual feelings can be the loudest call from the inner man, calling out for wholeness, satisfaction, sense of belonging, to be one and complete with someone who understands life better. It is that urge to pull up the outer clothes, rip the body and find a way that takes you to the real world inside. Sex is the best expression of what love is when it is understood from a spiritual point of *view*, it is the merging of two souls, opposite energies attracting each other to satisfy the emotional inner gap. That energy carries the power to bring forth what is in both souls, create a seed together and plant it, the seed will manifest into another soul. So sex is the best feeling ever, it has the capability to carry love but it is not love.

Love is a place of wholeness and satisfaction in the absence of anything material for it is a feeling that goes beyond the surface. Love is the mother of all the good and perfect emotion we can ever feel.

It is the energy that contains the ability to create things and bring them into existence. Like I mentioned earlier, emotion is energy in motion, therefore, love is the pure energy that flows from the highest place of Source for the purpose of giving life continuously. It is the DNA of God containing everything that is in God himself, as it flows, it is carrying the being of God. In other words, love is the Spirit of God, the life that proceeds from the Father to give life to everything that exists. It is that power which is translated into being by one who receives it.

We have heard of the Holy Trinity, the unity of God the Father, the Son and the Holy Spirit, the mystery of faith that helped me understand this subject of love. The bible tells us that God sent the Son into the world who then died, rose from the dead and went back to the Father where he then sent forth the Holy Spirit to the believers. This transactional process begins with God reaching out to his people in the plan of salvation for the purpose of reconciliation between God and mankind.

God is Spirit, for him to interact with mankind on earth he needed a physical body specifically prepared and molded to carry out his mission. The Son came as an incarnate expression of God's life on earth but he also remained God the Divine Spirit, this incarnated life was an extension of the Spirit of God putting on the user-friendly interface body required as he moves and operate in the world of mankind in order to carry out his mission. The body was for identification, for mankind to see him and talk to him in a manner in which is understandable. The Word became flesh and dwelt amongst us, the Word is the life of God, the Spirit of God, and the body was for earthly functionalities to enable him to speak his Word.

So the Son is the Spirit of God taking up the physical body, for God so loved the world that he gave his only begotten son...meaning when God loved, he came and dwelt amongst men. The Son was the embodiment of his love and his life was his expression of this love towards mankind. When he finished his works, in human point of view, he died and went back to the Father, in my spiritual perspective where God cannot die, he removed his physical body suit after a day's work, remember he is God of eternity, a day can be a thousand years.

So am I downplaying what happened to Christ in his physical therapy life? No, absolutely not, what takes place in both worlds is real and true from both angles of perspective, death was experienced on earth in the eyes of heaven and earth, just as resurrection took place in the eyes of men and heavenly world beyond. The Son of Man title implies that God had come as a man biologically, the same way every other men comes into this world.

Jesus was God the Father in a love relationship with mankind, and his Spirit was the gift of love packed inside, moving around touching lives, talking, expressing and revealing himself. He was a man in love.

Then when the salvation was accomplished by his physical death, the resurrection took place to demonstrate the existence of life beyond death, the eternity beyond physical life. There was no gap between physical and spiritual realities, God had come to merge the two worlds in order to allow the natural flow of love from the Father to his people he loved. The resurrection power is a gift of freedom to mankind that they may live and experience both worlds, they can now access the vaults of treasures in the spirit world and manifest them in the material world. Jesus Christ would enter through locked doors in his physical body to show off his Spirit body capabilities, he could sit and eat with them in his physical body capability. The day of resurrection was a Universe Union Day, celebrating the closing of the gap between worlds, the Universal reconciliation and freedom, the gates of heaven were opened for life to flow and fill the earth. Access is granted to those who become aware of the availability of this love life.

The Son ascended back to God the Father, in other words, the Spirit Life of God went out of the physical world having fulfilled his desire to reach out to his people and propose his love to them. He had laid down the fundamentals and introduced the basics of his kind of love through his teachings and activities in order to demonstrate his rich and wealthy, abundance and eternity lifestyle. He established this love through of his death and giving his own life to those who will accept his life. In death, he was breaking the chains that denied us access to life, he was delivering us from the kingdom of darkness into his marvelous light as it was in the beginning. What happened on the cross reveals to us how far and long the distance was between God and the world, the separation was so deep that men were way out of the alignment and were living in a troubled world of endless war, it projected the emotional inner gap. The cross was the ground breaking point where the body had to be broken to release the Life of God and let it flood the earth in abundance. He had to die so that his Holy Spirit, his breath of life can come down to fill the hearts of men in abundance.

Now God the Holy Spirit. There is a Catholic prayer to the Holy Spirit that helped me understand the third persona of God in the Holy Trinity. It is that power that raised Jesus from the dead, by his grace he performed those miracle and wonders. God, by the light of the Holy Spirit, he instructs the hearts of men, he fills hearts and lead them into faith and enkindle in them the fire of his love. This Spirit of God is the life of God from the beginning to end, the immortal life of God that lives forever. Therefore, when we encounter God in the Holy Spirit, we are meeting the same God who has been there all along, the Spirit that hovered above the waters, the Spirit that creates worlds.

And Jesus Christ told his disciples to wait for the Holy Spirit to come. On the day of Pentecost, God was now sealing his Spirit Life on his beloved people, filling their hearts with his love giving them full understanding of the things of life so that they can become aware of the eternal life and his gift of love. The purpose of his love that made him give his son to the world was to reveal himself to them and establish a relationship of love with them. Whosoever believed in the Son and his message of love will have eternal life. The coming of the Holy Spirit after the resurrection was the launching of the eternal life to the believers, restoring establishing the connection between God and men as it was in the beginning. He is that promise fulfilled in Christ as he expressed his love and he is that life he gave up on the cross that is now coming to the people he loved so that they can have eternal life and gain access to the kingdom treasures.

Holy Spirit is the power of love, the energy in motion towards the people, it is the emotional state of God and that energy is generated for the purpose of giving life continuously into eternity and beyond for it is life. By giving life, I mean it gives the ability to create, not only creating material things but also creating new understanding, the ability to evolve and expand towards improvement, to see better things, reaching for better side of life as it continue to unfold before us. The purpose of this energy is to create continuously, therefore, the universe will never stop evolving, it continues to expand as this energy keeps flowing, and as many receive this knowledge and energy, the more and faster the world evolves.

Love is the deepest desire in the centre of our being. Desire is stirred by what we see in the world of contrast where we see things and we compare and contrast preferences, sifting through things, what we want from what we don't want. We notice the gap and we want to close it. That is the desire to evolve towards love, the center of being which is the ultimate goal, to be where love is which is the place of God.

When we are connected to God, we become the embodiment of love, our hearts are filled with love and it is translated as energy to the brain and the brain is capable of generating the good feelings to the soul and body. Feeling good is everyone's heart's desire and it is ultimate reason we exist. All we want in everything we do is to feel good and be loved. Feeling good is what prepares the body and soul to be in the receptive mode of abundance, endless possibilities, life and love, purposes and destinies and so on.

Relationship with our source is what defines our way of life, knowing and understanding how to access the vaults of the kingdom of life that gives us the confidence of who we are. We realize our place in this universe and live within our purpose with zeal for life knowing we are connected to life itself and everything is supplied in abundance. Seek ye first the kingdom of God and everything else will be added unto you.

Take a deep breath and allow the love of God to flow through you for a moment. Feels good hey.

Personal Reflection Exercise

a) Find a quiet place and sit comfortably.

b) Close your eyes. Take a deep breath in and slowly breathe out, feel your body relax. Do it at least 3 times.

c) With your eyes closed, do the exercises in the end of Chapter 1 and 2.

d) Feel your heartbeat as you breathe in and out slowly. The heart is the central place of emotions where you can establish a point of supply of energy or life from the Source. As you breathe in, you are letting in the flow of life from within and breathing out releases this life into your world. As you keep deliberately taking in and releasing this life, it will fill your body and mind, that energy is what will become your magnetic field that will attract support from the universe, sending signals into space for intuitions insights, divine timings and networks, ideas and opportunities will flow effortlessly. Now that you have established your connection, you now know what love is, deliberately allow it to flow through you. Allow your heart to be the power- house of energy, where you generate power to create your world and manifest your dreams. As this energy flows through you, know that this energy is not yours to contain it therefore let it flow freely without controlling it. It is in abundance that you can never run dry, feel grateful that you were found aligned to the Source as its course flew in direction, your good energy field attracted the flow.

e) Say your prayers. And slowly bring back your mind and attention to your breath and slowly open your eyes

Chapter 7
Ask and It Is Given

"In that day you will ask in my name, and I do not say to you that I will ask the Father on your behalf, for the Father loves you'. John 16:26-27
"No one, after lighting a lamp puts it in a cellar or under a basket, but on a stand, so that those who enter may see the light.... If then your whole body is full of light, having no part dark, it will be wholly bright, as when a lamp with its rays gives light." Luke 11:33,36

As I come to one of the many conclusions of my endless inner conversations, here is my deepest conviction and confidence of all time:

SOURCE HAS MY BACK!

What is prayer and how should we pray? In other words, what is asking and how do we ask? To me prayer is being aware of our identity as a believer, understanding the character of God as the Father of all life and establishing a relationship with him to allow life to flow from the Source through us into the world around us. From that position, we are able to access the things available in the universe to help us along the way. As believers, we now know that there is no longer a gap between us and the source of life, he lives in us to prosper his plan through us, Christ is saying we are loved by the Father just as he is loved, therefore, we can now directly ask the Father to provide for us as we continuously seek his righteousness. Righteousness is what establishes our relationship with him, as we continue to show up before him showing that we are committed to fulfill what needs to be done, coming back for enlightenment on things we are struggling with as we go about in life, and we remain aligned and all things have no choice but to be added unto us, things will follow us on our way out into the world.

Life is all about energy and allowing it to flow through us. All we need is to ask, knock and seek for the inner path that is only true to us, and that path will always lead us to our Source of this energy which is life. Being aware of this place where we know all our prayers and requests are answered is the beginning of wisdom. As we go about in life trying to get the gist of what is going on, it is fine to face challenges and experience the unfairness and unfortunate events happening in life trusting the process anticipating the best at the end of it all. Those experiences stir in us the desire to expand and evolve for the better, to feel better, to reach for the better, to appreciate the better so that we can ask the Source to help us overcome and become an improved version of the current situation .

We will realize and acknowledge our current situation and get curious about the other side of that situation, we will be urged from within to close that gap. The desire to be better is the call from the inner being wanting to be free from the limitations of the physical environment, wanting more from life and better quality lifestyle, because the spirit is fully aware of the vastness and abundance in the world of immortality.

The desires and dreams we have at times feels like they are too good to be true and yet they are very much possible if we approach them perspective from which they are coming from. All we need is to acknowledge them and get them aligned to the Source who is the power that creates worlds and makes everything possible to conspire with the whole universe to deliver our desires.

Our part is to ask and to then receive, the source will always make the power available for us to turn thoughts and ideas into things. We have to develop the ability to receive from the Source, establish a channel of flow for the distribution of energy to take place. That power will then be translated into our desires depending on the receptive mode we are working on. So once we ask, the Source gives because that desire is actually conceived by the impulses from the Source, it is an inside job, we would not think and ask for what is outside the universe and beyond what the source can not give, it impossible. Therefore, our desires are already known and given, all we need is to ask and receive them.

It is us who create the gap between our desire and manifestation of it by not being aligned to the receiving environment. The power or energy is given to create what we want but along the way it can be wasted when we focus on the wrong things not serving the purpose of that desire we asked for, where focus is, the energy goes, if we lose focus we also lose the flow of energy, there is discord between the giver and the receiver. When we ask, let's allow ourselves to receive and fine tune our receiving frequency by focusing and tuning in for insights, impulses, ideas, being channeled through as a process to manifest desires into reality.

There is a journey in between desire and manifestation which is traveled towards manifestation as everything come together, the whole universe conspire and work together to bring forth our desires. As we travel it we need to enjoy the fun of working things out, trusting the universe to deliver the desires, having fun as the universe put in the details of the manifestation into reality as unfolds before us. It is obvious that we won't enjoy the idea of having things falling instantly from the sky. We would want the details of buying a lottery ticket to manifest a million dollars, or a donor coming through for me to manifest an electric wheelchair. It won't feel good to see it falling out of nowhere for me, we want the consignment details in order to feel good and better at the end of the manifestation. That was the reason why God took his time in molding the structure of a man out of the dust or clay with his own hands, he was adding the details of the his idea and concept as he envisioned in his mind.

The conviction and assurance that everything is working out for the good for us is real, the Source has our back when we are know who we are in the Kingdom, the same God who desired and loved the world so much that he gave his only begotten son is the same God who came as the Son to manifest himself in the physical world, he is the same God that comes in the Holy Spirit as the promise of his love to fulfill it by sealing his Spirit Life on us so that our bond and union with him is established to live happily forever after.

In John 10.10, he says I came that they may have life , life in abundance, all we now have to do is to position ourselves in alignment with God, define our life, decide on what we want and declare it for delivery!

Personal Reflection Exercise

a) Find a quiet place and sit comfortably.

b) Close your eyes. Take a deep breath in and slowly breathe out, feel your body relax. Do it at least 3 times.

c) With your eyes closed, do the exercises in the end of Chapter 1 and 2.

d) As you allow the love energy to flow through you, remember that this love is coming from your creator, the creator of all things. It is that Power that created all that you see around. You are living in a world that was once void and empty and everything was called forth and came into existence. What calls forth things into being are your desires being aligned to this energy that creates worlds. Become aware that you are an extension of what God wants to work out and as you are his idea, your desires, prayers, visions, passions and dreams are launched as rockets from the deepest of your soul inside to the surface for you to realize them and your job is to receive them into your realization because, as you know that with God nothing is impossible, his answers are always yes and amen. Now that the Spirit of God is within us Jesus said you no longer need him to ask on your behalf for the Father loves you just as he loves him so you now have direct access to him. Asking in his name is asking in the spirit of Jesus Christ, that same Spirit that understands life from the physical world side of things, that same Spirit who became flesh and dwelt amongst men, he will grant accordingly and abundantly for he knows all your needs and desires. Believe that you are in this world not on your own but for the life of he who lives forever, always give thanks for the opportunity to desire to evolve and expand, keep wanting more and better. The spirit of life will flow effortlessly towards you to help you manifest your dreams.

e) Say your prayers. And slowly bring back your mind and attention to your breath and slowly open your eyes

Epilogue

As I was writing this book, my thoughts were, is it really necessary for me to write a book about these personal conversations? Who would really consider reading a book from me? The thought of it made me feel pity for myself. Inspirational books can be very controversial and confusing, so I could be wasting my time. These and many other thoughts kept coming to support one another as they were conspiring against the idea of writing the book!

But I went to the other side of these thoughts, wanted to see what was going on there before I give up. I saw myself setting a wonderful record in my family by being the first to write and publish a book. I think I once heard that my father had a book he was in the process of writing whilst he was a teacher but he never published it, he would be so proud of me. I thought of that only one person who would read this book and catch the fire of it and resonate with it, and be filled with life as it flows while reading page after page of pure inspiration. Above all, just the thought of me writing an entire book is what just excites me the most because the major challenge I faced in life due to my disability was that I could not hold a pen to write on my own therefore I was not able to write at all. But here I am, I have come this far to be here, think of defying the odd one by one, writing and publishing a book is just one of a kind. Wouldn't it feel wonderful to appear on one of those prestigious events and be called to the stage and be introduced as : "Let me now call upon Miss Mollen Garikai to the stage, the author of the best-selling book ....." And I would narrate my story of how I lived my life against all odds and reached my potential beyond my limitations... So many others thoughts came as well to conspire together in supporting the idea of writing the book.

Given both sides, I would choose one from the other everyday depending on the type of energy I will be allowing to flow that day, at times I would allow self-doubt, unworthy, low self-esteem and limiting beliefs to take me for days and I would not feel inspired to write at all. Other times I would allow good vibes to come through and the inspiration and insights would just flow as I was writing the book. It was a matter of choice, choosing which side to focus on. It was not the lack of words to put together in writing or inspiration but what thoughts I will be allowing into my mind. Where focus goes, energy flows and what we think about, the universe brings about too.

In his book, Science of Mind, Ernest Holmes says, and I quote: "Since we can all conceive of a greater good than we have so far experienced, we all have the ability to transcend previous experiences and rise triumphant over them." The universe awaits for those who dare to ask for more out of it, those who are aware of the vastness of the universe and hungry to explore it experience the power of God as they allow it to flow with it regardless of their physical conditions and circumstances. We are coming from Source and going back, we all have direct access to the Source. The difference is in the levels of awareness and how we are aligned to the Source who is God within us. We no longer wait to go to heaven to see the power and the glory, the kingdom has come and we now carry it.

The stream of his power is flowing, let's dive in and go with it!

Don't miss out!

Visit the website below and you can sign up to receive emails whenever Mollen Garikai publishes a new book. There's no charge and no obligation.

https://books2read.com/r/B-A-KHEW-JQZDC

BOOKS 2 READ

Connecting independent readers to independent writers.

About the Author

Mollen Garikai is an Internet Entrepreneur, Online Business Expert, Digital Marketer and disability Lifestyle Blogger.

Although she is a woman with a disability, she's purpose-driven, determined to unleash her potential to realize her dreams and to help others to do the same.